AF228953

WOMEN IN *Music*

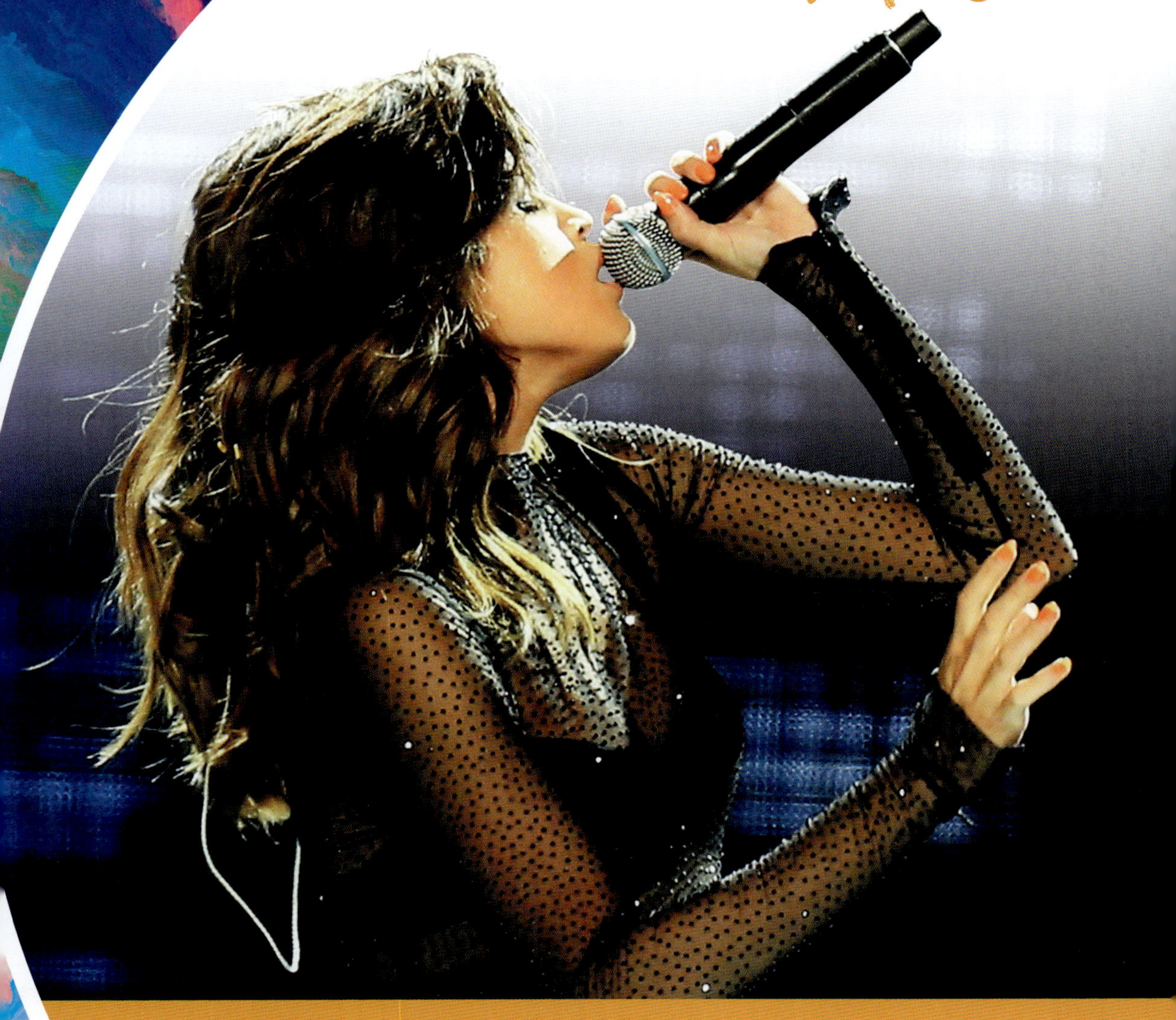

BY ROBERTA BAXTER

CONTENT CONSULTANT
Cynthia Green Libby
Professor
Music Department
Missouri State University

Cover image: Selena Gomez often sings about the joys and sorrows of love.

Core Library

An Imprint of Abdo Publishing
abdopublishing.com

abdopublishing.com

Published by Abdo Publishing, a division of ABDO, PO Box 398166, Minneapolis, Minnesota 55439. Copyright © 2019 by Abdo Consulting Group, Inc. International copyrights reserved in all countries. No part of this book may be reproduced in any form without written permission from the publisher. Core Library™ is a trademark and logo of Abdo Publishing.

Printed in the United States of America, North Mankato, Minnesota
022018
092018

Cover Photo: Don Arnold/WireImage/Getty Images
Interior Photo: Don Arnold/WireImage/Getty Images, 1; 13thWitness/Invision for Parkwood Entertainment/AP Images, 4–5; John Shearer/WireImage/Getty Images, 8–9, 43; Chelsea Purgahn/The Daily Texan/AP Images, 11, 45; Matteo Chinellato/Shutterstock Images, 14–15; Robert Gauthier/Los Angeles Times/Getty Images, 18; Red Line Editorial, 19, 30; Joan Leong/AP Images, 22–23; Ron Galella/WireImage/Ron Galella Collection/Getty Images, 25; Shutterstock Images, 26; John Salangsang/Invision/AP Images, 28–29; Ondrej Deml/CTK/AP Images, 34–35; Ayrton Vignola/Agencia Estado/AP Images, 38

Editor: Marie Pearson
Imprint Designer: Maggie Villaume
Series Design Direction: Claire Vanden Branden

Library of Congress Control Number: 2017962830

Publisher's Cataloging-in-Publication Data

Names: Baxter, Roberta, author.
Title: Women in music / by Roberta Baxter.
Description: Minneapolis, Minnesota : Abdo Publishing, 2019. | Series: Women in the arts | Includes online resources and index.
Identifiers: ISBN 9781532114779 (lib.bdg.) | ISBN 9781532154607 (ebook)
Subjects: LCSH: Women in music--Juvenile literature. | Women musicians--Juvenile literature. | Sound recording executives and producers--Juvenile literature. | Women in the performing arts--Juvenile literature.
Classification: DDC 782.4216409--dc23

CONTENTS

CHAPTER
ONE

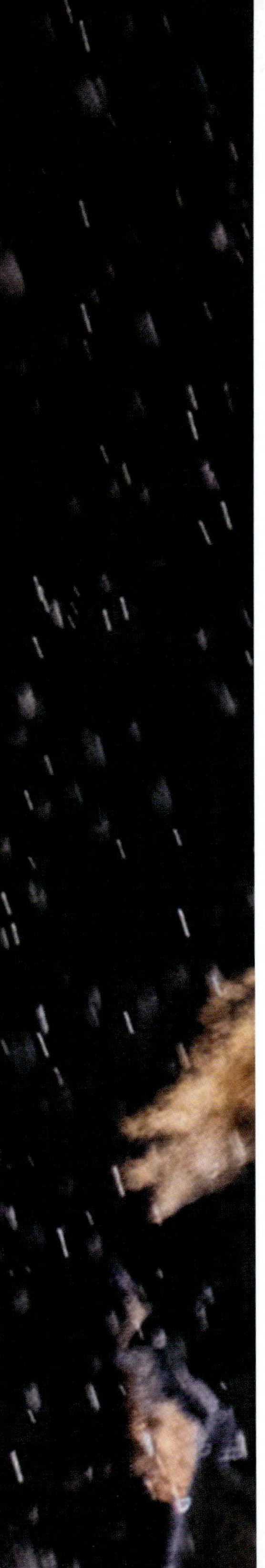

Beyoncé's Lemonade

Beyoncé strode onto the stage in a lemon-yellow outfit, microphone in hand, kicking up water that covered the stage. She performed for an hour, singing her hits from her latest album, *Lemonade*. It was April 27, 2016, in Miami, Florida. This first stop was the start of her Formation World Tour. Beyoncé was overjoyed when fans began singing the words of the song "Hold Up." *Lemonade* had been out for only five days, but fans already knew the words.

Lemonade, both the video and concert performance, dazzles with music and images.

Beyoncé and dancers splashed in the water onstage during her Formation World Tour.

It includes songs about the pain of trauma and betrayal. Dream-like scenes are woven with music to create an emotional experience. The music can be heard alone or in music videos that show the powerful scenes Beyoncé created. The first week the album came out in 2016, it hit Number 1 on *Billboard's* 200 most popular albums. Beyoncé was the first artist to have her first six albums each hit the Number 1 spot.

WORLDWIDE STAR

The Formation World Tour promoted the album *Lemonade* around the world. More than 2.2 million fans bought tickets to see Beyoncé. The tour brought in $256 million.

Beyoncé has astonished her fans and the music world since she began performing. She's not the only one. Other women succeed in singing, performing, and writing music of all kinds. They bring their own special touches to music around the world.

Explore Online

Chapter One discusses Beyoncé's *Lemonade*. The website below explores how her album relates to current events. As you know, every source is different. What information does the website give about the album? How is the information from the website the same as the information in Chapter One?

Beyoncé's Lemonade Is Defiant in the Midst of Upheaval
abdocorelibrary.com/women-in-music

Rocking the Industry

Rock music often uses a strong beat and electric instruments. Men once dominated rock. But more women have been making a name in it. And they are using new platforms to do it. Avril Lavigne had a big hit with her third album in 2007. She both wrote and performed the song "Girlfriend." The song deals with Lavigne's frustration of liking a boy but not liking his girlfriend. The video makes watchers cheer as the girlfriend trips into a pool at a miniature golf course. The boy winds up with Lavigne as

Avril Lavigne performed "Girlfriend" at the 2007 Teen Choice Awards.

Madonna has been a famous female artist since the 1980s. She has been a big influence on women in music. Many of today's stars say she inspired them to be musicians. She was the first woman to control every part of a performance—music, costumes, video, and production. Her music celebrates women and their strengths. Her songs draw from pop, disco, and even ballads. She was inducted into the Rock and Roll Hall of Fame in 2008. In 2013 the World Music Awards called her the most "influential female recording artist of all time."

his new girlfriend. This music video was the first YouTube video to reach 100 million views.

GUITARISTS AND SONGWRITERS

Thao Nguyen is a singer and songwriter. She is also the lead musician for the group Thao & The Get Down Stay Down. They released their fourth album, *A Man Alive*, in 2016. Nguyen sings and plays guitar. She taught herself to play as a child, and she is

Nguyen is known for her guitar skills and sometimes-throaty voice.

now an expert guitarist. Her fingers fly as the notes soar from her guitar.

Tracks, or single songs, on the album expose the troubles people all carry inside themselves but don't show. For Nguyen the emotional pain came from being abandoned by her father. He left her family when she was young. This theme is woven into the songs in *A Man Alive*.

The song "Nobody Dies" expresses a child's hurt and longing for someone who has left. The tracks offer both anger and forgiveness. The music uses close harmonies and discordant notes with a strong rhythm.

Another woman driving the rock industry is Kaki King. She is a guitarist and composer who performs jazz-based music. She wrote all the songs on the album *Everybody Loves You*. The songs are all instrumental. King plays the guitar with a style she developed herself. She plays so many notes with her powerful strumming that it sounds like two guitars in some places. Drumming on the guitar adds a strong beat. King helped write the soundtrack for the 2007 film *Into the Wild*. The soundtrack was nominated for a Golden Globe award in 2008.

Pop Superstars

Pop musicians compose the kind of music that is heard on the radio and sticks in people's heads. Many perform songs that go from wild joy to soft despair. Some women who sing pop music are known for their wild costumes.

Lady Gaga is especially famous for her vivid costumes and big voice that can belt out the songs. Exaggerated shoulder pads, crystals, and thick platform shoes are just some styles she's used. She's been covered in bubbles, human hair, and a giant eggshell. She's also appeared as a tooth fairy. She wears costumes so often that some fans don't know what she really looks like.

Lady Gaga changed costumes 15 times in each show during her 2010 Monster Ball tour.

Selena Gomez released her first solo album in 2013. Her music quickly became popular. Her songs encourage women and girls around the world. She generally makes music in the pop genre, though she has worked with other artists to make electronic music as well. In 2017 *Billboard* named her Woman of the Year.

Lady Gaga's first big hit was "Just Dance." Worldwide, fans sang the song for weeks, and it hit Number 1 on the pop charts. She wrote and performed this song and many others on her albums. In 2015 Lady Gaga received the first ever Contemporary Icon Award from the Songwriters Hall of Fame.

DREAMER

Katy Perry is a pop singer and songwriter. Similarly to Lady Gaga, she has created a strong image around herself. She has also earned many honors. In 2010 she released the album *Teenage Dream*. Five songs on that album hit Number 1. Perry was the first woman and second artist to achieve this. Her tour reflected the sugary feel the album had. She wore colorful dresses and wigs and decorated the stage with lollipops. In 2012 *Billboard* named Perry Woman of the Year. Many of Perry's songs make fans want to dance.

YOUNGEST SOLO ARTIST

One of the best-selling artists in recent years is Rihanna. She was born in Barbados, an island in the Caribbean. Her music reflects the strong rhythm and musical culture of her country. The beat is not only heard but also felt through the songs. Her first album, *Music of the Sun*, went to the Top 10 of the *Billboard* 200 in 2005. Rihanna was only 17 years old when she recorded the album. She is the youngest solo artist to have 14 Number 1 singles on the *Billboard* Hot 100.

"Firework"

Katy Perry's song "Firework" is from her *Teenage Dream* album. Perry hopes the song will make people feel proud and strong. She calls it her "one song." If she could only sing one song, it would be "Firework" because she likes its beat and positive message.

Rihanna, *center*, performed with Kanye West, *right*, and Paul McCartney at the 2015 Grammy Awards.

Rihanna released her eighth album, *Anti*, in 2016. One song, "Work," hit Number 1 on the charts in just a few weeks. It mixes a dancehall beat with rhythm and blues (R & B) and hip-hop. It also has a moody feel. The song is about struggling in a relationship. Rihanna sings words commonly used in the Caribbean, reflecting her roots in the area.

VIEWS AS OF JANUARY 2018

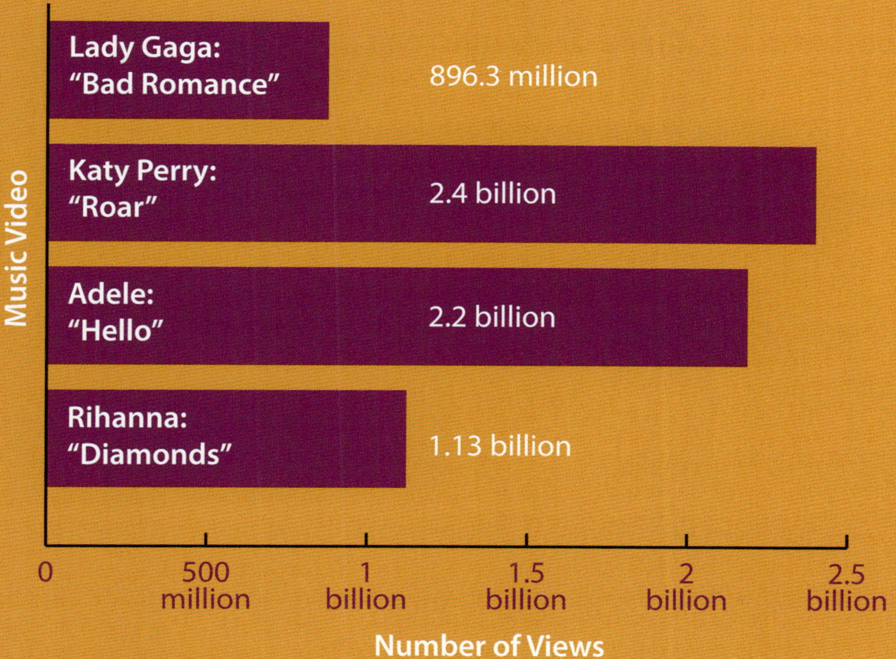

Women in pop not only have strong sales in albums and singles. Their music videos also have millions and billions of views. This chart shows how many views a few music videos by female artists have on YouTube. Why do you think some have more views than others?

ACROSS THE OCEAN

Adele stands out in pop music. She doesn't have vivid costumes. She usually wears an elegant dress for an entire concert. Her voice can be strong and bold and then soft and whispery. Adele grew up in a single-parent household in the United Kingdom. Her songs reflect both the struggles of life and the fun, bright side.

She was the first woman in *Billboard* history to have three Top 10 singles at one time. She also had two Top 10 albums as well as two Top 10 singles on the charts at the same time. Her album *21* broke a record on April 6, 2017. It had remained on the *Billboard* 200 list for 319 weeks in a row. One famous track is "Someone Like You." It is an emotional song about a breakup with a boyfriend. The sorrowful simplicity of the song connected with many listeners.

In 2011 tragedy struck. Adele injured her vocal cords. She had to stop singing for months. After surgery she was able to return to performing. But in 2017, she reinjured her vocal cords. She has also said she doesn't enjoy touring and may never tour again.

STRAIGHT TO THE
SOURCE

Lady Gaga explained why she tends to wear bold or crazy outfits when she performs:

> *I would say that I am [insecure]. Maybe it's from the things I experienced in my past, you know? Being beautiful is not so fun when you're in a business with all men. . . . It can actually get in the way. So in some ways, the outfits—these creations are because I don't want to face the reality of what people want from a female pop star. Everybody always laughs because I feel so much more comfortable with, like, a giant paper bag on my whole body and paint on my face. Sometimes I try really hard to take it all off. But inevitably what's underneath is still not a straight edge. And I don't think it ever will be.*

> Source: Andy Cohen. "The Monster Talent: Lady Gaga." *Glamour*. Condé Nast, October 29, 2013. Web. Accessed October 17, 2017.

What's the Big Idea?

Take a close look at this passage. What is the connection Lady Gaga is making between the male-dominated music industry and her clothing choices? What does it seem that some people want from a female pop star according to this excerpt?

Rap/Hip-Hop and R & B

Rap and hip-hop music use strong beats and rhythmic speech set to music. R & B music often combines feelings of sadness with African-American folk music. It is put to a beat with simple music. Each of these genres grew out of music created by African Americans. African-American artists continue to drive both genres.

RAPPER, SONGWRITER, PRODUCER

Hip-hop began with almost all male artists. Then Missy Elliott began writing and producing songs in the 1990s. She wrote her first hit,

Missy Elliott is known for her clever rhymes and her dance moves in music videos.

"That's What Little Girls Are Made Of," for a young Raven-Symoné in 1993.

Elliott released her own first album, *Supa Dupa Fly*, in 1997. Elliott broke through the male-dominated field of hip-hop. She was the first woman to write and rap an entire album. Her first album used unusual rhythms, touches of blues harmonies, and strong drums to create powerful music. It is still considered one of the best hip-hop records ever.

Her next albums also topped the charts. In 2002 she released the album *Under Construction*. She teamed up with Beyoncé on one song. Elliott is the only female rapper with six certified-platinum albums. That means each album sold at least 1 million copies.

Raven-Symoné released her first music in 1993.

She continues to write and produce for other artists as well as herself.

JENNIFER LOPEZ

Jennifer Lopez, known as J.Lo, is famous for her hits in music and for starring in films. She grew up in a Puerto Rican household in New York. Her family listened to

music with Caribbean flavor as well as hip-hop, pop, jazz, and R & B. She took singing and dancing lessons. She worked with singer Janet Jackson and can be seen in some of Jackson's videos.

Lopez's first album was *On the 6*, out in 1999. In 2000 her single, "Waiting for Tonight," made *Billboard* Hot 100's Top 10. Her music is sometimes smooth and slow. Other songs make listeners want to dance. Her style is popular. She has had four songs hit Number 1 on *Billboard's* Hot 100.

Ebony Naomi Oshunrinde is a Canadian rap music producer known as WondaGurl. She learned to produce music from the Internet. While she was in high school in 2012, she produced the song "Crown" for rapper Jay-Z. After that project, she continued to make beats at home after she finished her homework. Her family is Nigerian. The dancehall music popular with her family influenced her work.

Jennifer Lopez mixes catchy tunes with energizing dance moves.

CHAPTER
FIVE

Country Twang

Country music comes from styles popular with cowboys in the American West. Women have been present in country music for a long time. Today some are known around the world.

One of the biggest names in country music is Taylor Swift. She loved music from an early age. When she was 14 years old, her family moved to Nashville, Tennessee, so she could try to star in country music. She started writing songs and learning about the business. Many times her work was discounted because she was a young woman. But she kept on writing and singing.

Taylor Swift got her start in country, but today she writes and performs pop.

TAYLOR SWIFT ALBUMS, FIRST WEEK SALES

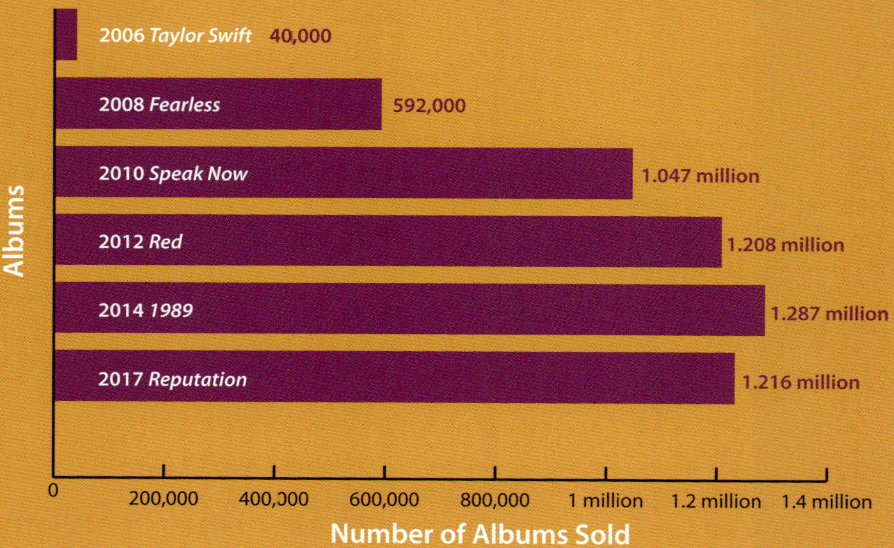

Taylor Swift's last four albums have each sold more than 1 million copies the first week after their releases. What do you think influenced how many albums sold the week after their releases?

Her first album, *Taylor Swift*, came out in 2006. It had a song called "Teardrops on My Guitar." The song was about her struggle with liking a boy when he liked another girl. Girls all around the world knew that feeling. Swift's album made her a star. She had helped write the song, and she sang and played guitar on the track.

During the next eight years, Swift recorded three more country albums. Those albums sold well. Her popularity continued to rise. In 2014 Swift decided she wanted to make her music more pop than country. Her album *1989* went to the top of the charts. The video of the song "Shake It Off" featured fans chosen from social media and fan letters. That year Swift became the first artist to have three albums sell 1 million copies in a week. She also became the first woman to win the Grammy Album of the Year twice.

WINNER TWICE OVER

Carrie Underwood loved to sing. But she studied broadcast journalism in college. Her life changed when she tried out for the

Swift faced challenges and skepticism about her change from country music to pop. Even people on her own team thought it was a mistake. They also questioned the name of the album, *1989*. That was the year when Swift was born. But she pushed forward. They soon found out that Swift had made a smart move. The album sold nearly 1.29 million copies in its first week.

TV show *American Idol*. She won this singing competition show in 2005. That win launched her career in country music.

Her first album, *Some Hearts*, was released in 2005. It became the fastest-selling female country record since the Nielsen SoundScan system began keeping track of sales in 1991. She went on to have other top-selling albums.

In 2008 the Grand Ole Opry made Underwood a member. The Opry promotes and preserves country music. Underwood was the youngest person to ever receive that honor. That year she also won the Country Music Award for top female vocalist for the third time.

In 2015 Underwood released a new album, *Storyteller*. She helped write some of the songs. The songs are about things all people can feel. In one song, "Heartbeat," a boyfriend and girlfriend leave the busy city to enjoy the quieter outdoors. They appreciate seeing fireflies and other things they can't find in the city.

CHAPTER
SIX

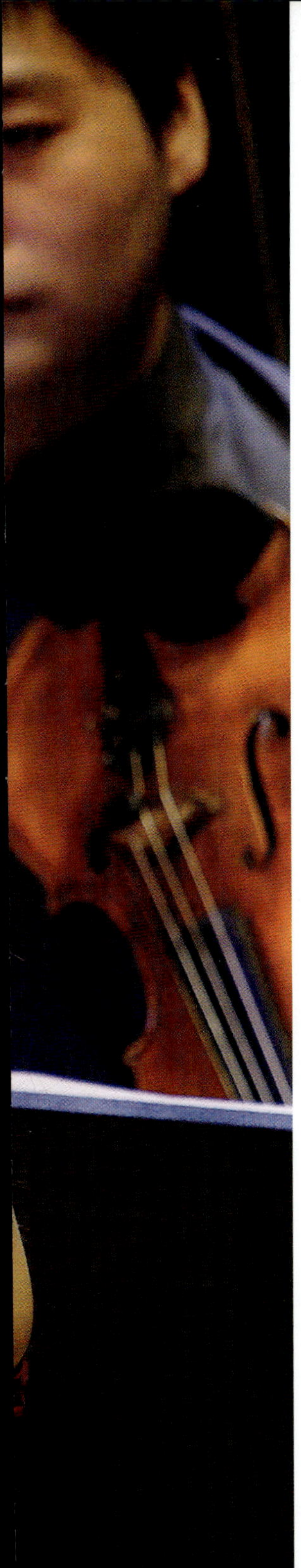

Mastering Classical Music

Classical music is played by large groups of people in an orchestra or symphony. A chamber orchestra is a small orchestra that plays similar music. Some classical musicians play music written by composers from long ago, such as Ludwig van Beethoven. Others play music written by contemporary composers.

The world of classical music has been especially resistant to women in many areas. In a survey of American orchestras, only 1.8 percent of the music played from

Sarah Chang first performed at age eight with the New York Philharmonic and has gone on to a successful performing career.

2014 to 2015 was by female composers. Of the world's 150 top conductors, only five were women. But some women have risen to fame in classical music.

SOLO VIOLINIST

Sarah Chang is Korean-American. Her father plays violin, so she learned violin as a child. When she was six, she won a scholarship to the famous Juilliard School and learned about music.

When she was eight years old, she performed music by Italian violinist Niccolò Paganini. She played alongside another famous violinist and the

New York Philharmonic orchestra. Soon she was playing as a solo violinist with orchestras around the world. She says that people who perform or listen to classical music know good music when they hear it. They don't go in for special effects or fluff. Everyone is expected to play well. She practices daily to be the best.

She is known for excellent playing of Paganini, Mendelssohn, and Tchaikovsky concertos. During one performance, a critic praised her range of notes. She played very low and then so high that the notes could barely be heard. She has also recorded several albums with different orchestras.

CONDUCTING

Marin Alsop is the music director of the Baltimore Symphony Orchestra and the São Paulo Symphony Orchestra. She is the first woman to be the main conductor of a major American orchestra.

Alsop's parents were both professional classical musicians. She grew up in a musical home. She decided

at an early age that she wanted to conduct orchestras. She studied at Yale University and Juilliard School. A high point for her was studying with famous conductor Leonard Bernstein. She also plays jazz violin.

In 1993 Alsop got her first position as a conductor of an American orchestra. The Colorado Symphony hired her. Her expertise led that orchestra to earn awards. Orchestras around the world wanted her to conduct concerts. Eventually she joined the Baltimore Symphony Orchestra.

She was also the conductor of a music festival in London, England. It is called the Last Night of the Proms. In 2015 she chose to feature a contemporary piece by a woman, Eleanor Alberga. Alberga was born in Jamaica, and she composed music with a female theme. *Arise, Athena* was inspired by the Greek goddess Athena. The music tells the story of a peaceful world that is attacked by some unknown force.

Alsop and the São Paulo Symphony Orchestra have performed across Europe.

The people call on the goddess Athena to restore order to the world. It begins quietly with melodies that don't seem to fit together. The sound rises in until drums pound, low brass notes rise quickly, and people sing, "Arise, Athena!" The melodies combine and soften to a sweet flute solo. Then brass and drums build up again to a quick finish.

Women have faced difficulties in all types of music. But they have kept on writing, singing, and performing excellent music. Millions of fans around the world enjoy their work every day.

STRAIGHT TO THE
SOURCE

Professional classical musicians must all practice individually and as part of a group. In an interview, Sarah Chang talked about how important practice has been to her musical career:

When I was very young, my parents ensured that my education was non-stop. I practiced the piano, then practiced the violin, then practiced gymnastics, and so on. I really had no idea that I would turn out as a violinist. . . . When I was younger, I focused on the violin part alone, and tried simply to conquer it. Now I look at the entire orchestral score [written music], to get a picture of what everyone is doing. Many young artists these days would like to be both soloist and conductor, but that is not for me. I just want to examine everything in the work so I can play it completely.

Source: "An Interview with Violinist Sarah Chang." Vancouver Classical Music. Geoffrey Newman, 2011. Web. Accessed October 17, 2017.

Consider Your Audience

Adapt this passage for a different audience, such as your parents, music teacher, or friends. Write a blog post conveying this same information for the new audience. How does your post differ from the original text and why?

NOTABLE WORKS

Teenage Dream—Katy Perry

Katy Perry's *Teenage Dream* was the first album by a woman to have five Number 1 hits. One of the songs, "Firework," is an upbeat rhythmic piece. The title song, "Teenage Dream," is a love song describing the first love that teenagers feel.

A Man Alive—Thao Nguyen

Thao Nguyen wrote her album *A Man Alive* with the emotions she felt from being abandoned by her father. The tracks express both anger and forgiveness. The music moves from close harmonies to discordant notes with a strong underlying rhythm.

"Work"—Rihanna

"Work" is a top-selling single on Rihanna's album *Anti.* The song mixes a dancehall beat with R & B and hip-hop. It has a moody feel. The repetition of the word *work* adds to the feel of frustration and endless work.

Arise, Athena—Eleanor Alberga

Eleanor Alberga's composition *Arise, Athena* features a variety of solo instruments. The piece begins with a chaotic sound that grows louder until people sing, "Arise, Athena!" The music becomes more unified and softens to a flute solo, and then brass and drums build up again to a quick finish.

STOP AND THINK

Tell the Tale

Chapter Three explores costumes and props some pop artists use at concerts. Imagine you are attending these concerts. Write 200 words about the costumes and stage setups you see. How are the fans behaving when the artists come onstage?

Dig Deeper

After reading this book, what questions do you still have about women in music? With an adult's help, find a few reliable sources that can help you answer your questions. Write a paragraph about what you learned.

Say What?

Learning about different kinds of music can mean learning a lot of new vocabulary. Find five words in this book you've never heard before. Use a dictionary to find out what they mean. Then write the meanings in your own words, and use each word in a new sentence.

Why Do I Care?

You may never join the music industry. But women in music are still changing the world. How are women proving that they can perform just as well as men? Would you want to listen to music performed by only men or only women?

GLOSSARY

composer
someone who writes music

concerto
a piece of classical music that highlights a solo or several solos with an orchestra

conductor
the person who leads an orchestra

discordant
sounds that create tension

genre
a category of music based on certain sounds or styles

harmony
a combination of notes that sound good together

melody
a pleasing sequence of notes

orchestra
a large group of people who play classical music on instruments

rhythm
the pattern of beats in music

symphony
a piece of music written for an orchestra; also, a large group that plays classical music

vocal cords
the parts of the throat that help people speak or sing

ONLINE RESOURCES

To learn more about women in music, visit our free resource websites below.

Visit **abdocorelibrary.com** for free Common Core resources for teachers and students, including vetted activities, multimedia, and booklinks, for deeper subject comprehension.

Visit **abdobooklinks.com** for free additional online weblinks for further learning. These links are routinely monitored and updated to provide the most current information available.

LEARN MORE

Dickinson, Stephanie E. *Katy Perry*. New York: Cavendish Square, 2015.

Griffiths, Katie. *Rihanna*. New York: Cavendish Square, 2015.

McCarthy, Cecilia Pinto. *The Science of Music*. Minneapolis, MN: Abdo, 2017.

INDEX

About the Author

Roberta Baxter has written numerous books about history and science for students of all ages. She enjoys listening to all kinds of music and once played in the school band. She lives in Colorado.